COMING OUT & COVERING UP:

CATHOLIC PRIESTS TALK ABOUT SEX SCANDALS IN THE CHURCH

by

Lisa Rene Reynolds, PhD

John P. Rutledge, Editor

ACKNOWLEDGMENTS

Thank you to the entire Dead End Street® team, for their belief in this work, and to the PhD faculty at Nova Southeastern University, especially my dissertation chair Dr. Chris Burnett, for teaching me about the research process and helping me to understand and eventually love mixed-methodology studies.

My gratitude to Dr. Barry Duncan and Dr. Scott Miller, for influencing my interviewing style and for the many opportunities you afforded me to write.

Appreciation also goes out to Father Mario Julian, for his willingness to clarify terms and themes for me as they surfaced throughout the research and writing process, and to my friends Ginny Flynn and Mary Katherine DiModugno for our enlightening conversations.

A special thanks to my parents, for their unwavering faith, and to my uncle Ken, for keeping me on-track, and husband Scott, for his endless computer assistance.

And I can't forget my three daughters — Ashley, Emma and Claire; thank you for giving me a new purpose and meaning, a depth of love beyond description, and the energy to do anything.

Most importantly, of course, thanks be to God for everything good.

CONTENTS

INTRODUCTION

Dr. Reynolds has made an important contribution to understanding the priesthood at this troubled time. She puts flesh on the statistical bones with her sensitive and moderate reactions to the respondents. While she makes no claim that her research represents probability sampling from which one could generalize to the whole body of the priesthood, her respondents "feel" much like those in the major surveys I have worked with in recent years.

Her respondents are good men under great pressure. I wanted originally to call my book on the subject *Priests in the Pressure Cooker* because the pressures on priests from the sex abuse scandal, shortage of priests, overwork, unreasonable demands from the laity, and insensitivity of those in authority are enormous. Yet like most of us, Dr. Reynolds' priests are going to stick it out.

Far more qualitative research like this will be necessary if laity are to understand priests and priests are to understand themselves. I would like to know who the priests are who continue to recruit others to follow them and why other priests have given up recruiting. Maybe this can be Dr. Reynolds' next project.

Perhaps the strongest asset of this work is that, unlike so many of the laity, the author is sympathetic to our human faults and failings. The idealized image of the priesthood that many of the laity still entertain is cruel and unfair. Priests are, as the Epistle of the Hebrews says, taken from among humans so that when they offer sacrifice for the sins of the people they also sacrifice for their own sins.

Father Andrew Greeley, PhD • May 21, 2004
Best-selling author of *The Priestly Sins* and *Cardinal Sins*

PREFACE

Dr. Reynolds has provided a breath of fresh air in the often-acrid and sometimes-stale atmosphere of dry statistics and seemingly endless media coverage of the Catholic Church's recent sex scandals. She offers a remarkably candid snapshot of ordinary priests coping with post-scandal suspicions and challenges, of men genuinely concerned and anguished over the current state of the Catholic Church. Anger, loneliness, isolation, sexual issues, pastoral effectiveness, and concerns about vocations and the training of seminarians are all discussed with frankness and evident passion.

These priests openly admit that the Gospel is the heart of their message and ministry, and worry that parishioners have turned away from the Church because of its institutional sins and failings (and have thereby lost the presence of Jesus' merciful and saving love in their daily lives).

As a seminarian teacher for a quarter of a century (and now as a publisher of books meant to nourish the spirituality of the Catholic faith community), I am convinced that our present crisis is a great opportunity for renewal and revitalization with Christ at the center of our faith. I don't think anyone can come away from this book without a deeper understanding and realization that life in the priesthood is challenging and uniquely difficult.

Father Lawrence Boadt, C.S.P. • June 21, 2004
Publisher and President, Paulist Press

FOREWORD

Lisa Reynolds, in this excellent work, has filled a gap in the literature and commentaries arising out of the clerical child abuse scandal. It is time to listen to "the troops" who man the Church barricades, the priests who carry on their duties in an atmosphere of suspicion of – and, at times, hostility towards – the priesthood.

The Pontificate of Pope John Paul II has witnessed the progressive dismantling of the heterosexual priesthood and the ascendancy of the homosexual priesthood, containing within it a subculture characterized by the sexual abuse of young boys. As a result, the homosexualization of the priesthood and clerical abuse of young boys are facts that have now become imbedded in the consciousness of both clergy and laity. This situation is viewed with considerable alarm. Father Cozzens, former rector of St. Mary's Seminary in Cleveland, in his book *The Changing Face of the Priesthood,* states: "Straight men in a predominantly or significantly gay [seminary] environment commonly experience chronic destabilization." Robert McNally, writing in the Jesuit magazine *America,* cautions: "For decades we have been hearing stories about priestly training and religious houses that would have made Boccaccio blush." Further, in his book *Goodbye, Good Men,* Michael Rose writes:

> The trouble starts in the seminary, and gross sexual immorality and the protective network formed around that immorality, is only one of the major issues that needs to be forthrightly addressed by the Shepherds of the Catholic Church.

All of this has sparked a great deal of questioning within the structures of the Church and among active laity as to what extent, if any, there is a connection between the rising numbers of homosexual priests and the clerical molestation of young male children and teens. The Vatican itself begs the question in statements made by its high officials — declaring that homosexuals are not fit for the priesthood.

Is it even conceivable, as is now being bruited about, that this mega-pope, this media giant and international superstar who is touted as the greatest hands-on Pope in the Church's history, might one day become notorious because all this chaos happened on his watch?

The confusion and amazement among the clergy at the formal Church's disturbing lack of attention to its pedophilia and phebophilia problems, while the present Pontiff was still strong and vigorous, is baffling at the least and deeply disturbing at worst. This ongoing drama of a Church too slow to respond to its clerics' crimes against children makes me think the Church's structure needs some modernizing.

Just as I suspect the Iraqi prisoner abuse scandal does not stop with the soldiers in the photos, so this clerical condition surely does not lie solely with the lower ranks of the clergy. I find it ironic that the Church has suffered the greatest credibility problem in its storied history under a Pope who proclaims extreme certainty in his theological views. The consternation is, of course, reflected in the priesthood, making this book a one-of-a-kind in the growing genre of literature on child molestation in the priesthood. What does the "man in the trenches" think about all of this? How does he feel in the public eye when so much suspicion is cast on his brother-priests? What does he think is the future of the Catholic priesthood? These and many other questions are addressed and answered in this treasure trove of clerical reflections.

Father Patrick Bascio, PhD • May 25, 2004
Author of *A Crime of Innocence*, *The UN Was My Parish* and *The Failure of White Theology: A Black Theological Perspective*

A NOTE FROM THE AUTHOR

The idea for this book came from my own struggle to understand the escalation of sex scandals in the Catholic Church. Trying to be a good, practicing Catholic and raise my family in the same tradition has often left me confused and uneasy. Reading about the scandals and listening to the various dioceses' responses left me with too many unanswered questions and concerns. Speaking with my own priest proved informative and helpful, yet this was too narrow to be indicative of the larger population of priests living through this crisis. I wanted to hear more perspectives and experiences from those who deal daily with the repercussions of these scandals. Not from the Pope or the Bishop or their mouthpieces, but from the everyday clergy who work in local parishes; those who dedicate their lives to doing God's work. These are the people who hold the keys to understanding and change.

I used my graduate school research training to design a simple questionnaire that asked some of my deepest questions. I never expected the responses I received or the lengthy, personal revelations that accompanied the returned questionnaires.

What began as a personal quest for understanding turned out to be so much more. I was overwhelmed by the willingness of priests to be involved in this endeavor and amazed by the richness and depth of their thoughts and experiences. The clergy's insight was remarkable and I was left with some incredible grains of wisdom and a greater degree of comfort.

I am eternally grateful to the priests who chose to be involved in this project, and I thank each of them for their time and thoughtful, candid responses. Without their honesty and shared experiences, this book could never have been written. Through this exploration, I hope you find some new hope for the Church, a strengthened faith, and some consolation in the goodness that dwells within the bad.

Before we begin… a disclaimer and word of caution regarding this study and the information yielded: the experiences and themes portrayed here are not all-encompassing, nor do they represent any majority of opinion or sentiment. However, it does provide a beginning sample of an experience that has often been unknown by the public. The intent of this exploration was not meant to find an answer or solution, but rather to look for pieces that provide more knowledge and a better understanding.

A special thank you to Fr. Andrew Greeley, PhD and Father Patrick Bascio, PhD for their assistance and assessment of my work during its evolution.

I dedicate this book to the Catholic priests everywhere who do their jobs well everyday.

Lisa Rene Reynolds, PhD • June 10, 2004

THE STATE OF THE NATION

Our world has grown into a precarious place where greed, hatred and instability run rampant. From terrorism and youth violence, to an increased emphasis on material things, everyone has been touched in some way by the escalating fear of modern society. One need only look around their own neighborhood or social circle to see the state of things — the effects of divorce and abuse, the increasing rates of drug and alcohol dependence, and the prevalence of depression, anxiety and stress. The news media focuses on the most serious offenses, from mothers killing their own children to disgruntled ex-employees gunning down innocent office workers and our youth slaughtering one another at school. Indeed, our nation, our world feels decreasingly safe and secure.

One of the most poignant and disturbing trends to many people is the widespread allegations of sexual abuse to minors by Catholic clergymen. The media immediately highlights the cases and the news spreads like wildfire. The most recent reports (John Jay College of Criminal Justice, 2004) indicate that approximately 10,667 such allegations have been lodged. The Associated Press quotes David Clohessy (National Director of the Survivors Network of Those Abused By Priests) as saying this number is grossly understated because "thousands of victims haven't reported."

The number of clergy accused of perpetrating these sexual misdeeds translates to roughly 4% of the total number of clergy practicing in the nation during that time. Some feel that this percentage is insignificant given the 96% of priests that are presumably *not* molesting children. Others feel that one molesting priest is too many.

The misdeeds have been labeled pedophilia (the act or fantasy on the part of an adult of engaging in sexual activity with a child or children), hebephilia (a condition in which an adult, usually male, is sexually attracted to post-pubertal adolescents between 14 and 17 years of age), and phebophilia (a condition in which an adult, usually male, is sexually attracted to young people about the age of puberty); others simply call it sexual abuse. Regardless of how one chooses to classify these incidents, one thing remains clear — they are particularly unsettling because the Catholic clergy have traditionally ranked among the most trusted individuals; men to whom we bear our soul in confession. They are, Catholics believe, God's representatives on Earth, human beings ordained to put others before themselves to further God's work.

Perhaps over the years our society has set standards too high for these clergymen, forgetting that our clerics are mere mortals, human beings, faulty and imperfect, capable of weakness and even crime. Or maybe their indiscretions are among the greatest betrayals of all time. The emotions involved seem to be inseparable from the facts. I sought out to make this book an objective appraisal, an emotionless assessment, of the atrocities committed by otherwise good men. What I believe I ended up with was a collection of experiences that should serve as a wake-up call to us all. They are a testament to the state of our nation.

THE NORMAL RESPONSE TO CRISIS

My thirteen years of psychotherapy practice have focused on human responses to crisis and trauma. For the last year and a half, I have been actively and intimately involved in crisis counseling programs at schools, churches and parishes hit by a traumatic incident (e.g., murder, removal of a priest). The responses we see from people about the allegations of priesthood sexual misconduct and the subsequent "cover up" by officials are in many ways normative.

In response to shock or change, humans display signs of stress and adjustment — such things as anger, anxiety, sleeplessness, depression, frustration, loss of appetite and lack of energy. Much in the same way that parents sometimes have difficulty when their last child leaves home ("the empty nest syndrome"), people need time to react and adjust to changes. The old adage that "time heals" often holds true. However, in the case of scandal in the Church, people have not had a chance to heal and adjust due to the continual waves of new allegations.

As an immediate response, some people have chosen to leave the Church. Doubt and distrust give them the impetus to discontinue their involvement in the formal Church. As a psychotherapist, I find this decision quite curious, as these same people would assuredly not flee all future medical treatment if they experienced an isolated, yet traumatic incident with an individual physician. Rather, these people would most likely find a new physician and proceed with an increased level of caution. Why should the same not hold true for Catholics of their clergy? We must not lose sight of the "bigger picture."

We need to hear from the neglected voices of those at the forefront, those who live the priesthood experience every day, who know the stresses, frustrations and pressures inherent in clergy life. It is only through these voices and experiences that we might educate ourselves on the contributing factors and potential solutions to this parasitic problem in our religious hierarchy.

THE PLAN

The plan was simple: target the population most affected and rocked by scandal. I chose a county forced to deal with allegations of priesthood sexual misconduct in the last two years. I compiled a list of Catholic churches in that county and printed out the mailing address for each one. I addressed envelopes and enclosed self-addressed, stamped envelopes for return of the questionnaires. Everything was set to go. Now all I needed was the questionnaire.

The questions I selected were direct and varied. I kept it short (ten questions), hoping this would increase the response rate. I invited respondents to offer additional thoughts, ideas and viewpoints if they chose to do so.

I drafted a cover letter that described my experience and intent. I depicted my personal and professional concerns and asked the clergy to consider helping me gain a better understanding of the scandals. I explained my intent to write about the clergy's experiences, with the stated goal of representing this population of priests through their feedback and insight. I made it clear that the information gleaned from the survey would only be used in a respectful manner to facilitate the healing and support of apprehensive communities and individuals. I wanted the priests to know that their honesty would not appear in a sordid exposé, but rather an informative and enlightening exploration.

Though I assured the priests anonymity and requested no identifying information, the majority of respondents offered their names, enclosed notes on parish letterhead, and/or invited me to contact them with further questions.

The plan was to mail the questionnaires to each of the Catholic churches in the chosen county. The questionnaires were mailed in February 2003, and a few days later the responses began trickling in.

Of the 64 questionnaires sent out, 22 were completed and returned to me via mail. In addition, two priests initiated telephone contact and two recipients declined to participate, each saying he considered himself a "traditionalist" (and therefore not part of the current Vatican establishment). In layperson's terms, although legitimate practicing clergy, "traditionalists" do not believe in many of the updates and changes to current Church protocol (e.g., allowing females to be altar servers, no longer reciting scripture in Latin). Therefore, while these priests may head parishes and lead followers of God, they are estranged from the present-day hierarchy and do not collaborate or attend meetings with "modern" priests or guiding/governing Church bodies. These two traditionalists, although refusing to complete the questionnaire, did send a statement of their view on the current sex scandals (discussed later in this book).

THE RESULTS

Of the 64 questionnaires sent out, 26 responded in some form (a response rate of approximately 41%). Experts would label this rate "significant" (and therefore fairly indicative of this population's experience). The reader should be cautioned though — the nature of qualitative inquiry is to collect rich and detailed personal experiences. Therefore, although the numbers represent a good sampling of priests, this type of study can never assume it speaks to the experience of all priests.

As you will read, this inquiry reflects a wide range of experiences. Although they are one in their mission and life's work, priests are certainly very different in their thoughts, opinions and experiences.

The questions sent to the clergy were:

1. *Do you feel that the allegations… have made your job more difficult?*

Sixty-nine percent of the respondents answered yes. One priest specified that the difficulty was "not because of the people [parishioners], but due to my own inner turmoil [regarding the events]." Several other respondents echoed this viewpoint. And many described the extensive consoling and comforting requested by parishioners as a result of the misconduct.

A few priests felt that although the sex scandals have made their job more difficult, it was simply a *different* sort of difficulty than priests have traditionally faced. For example, one respondent reminded us that in times of war, priests are often asked to counsel grieving widows and mothers while simultaneously addressing parishioners' fears and anti-war demonstrations. Different pressures and demands, but no more difficult.

2. How many of your parishioners do you feel have used the allegations... as a reason or excuse to pull away from the Church or religion?

Fifty-eight percent responded that "at least a few" parishioners had pulled away from the Church as a result of the scandals and/or cover-ups. Others wrote that there were no departures "they definitively knew of," but that the allegations certainly could be the cause for any number of changes in parishioners' mass attendance or involvement. One respondent simply and eloquently wrote, "Who knows?"

Another added:

> We exist in a society and time that is rushed and overscheduled. It is difficult for people to make the commitment to come together in unity to worship. Truly, services, Sunday Mass, and holy days of obligation have become less of a priority in people's busy lives.

3. How concerned are you about the strength and stability of the parish you are currently at?

Fifty-two percent of the respondents expressed at least a little concern for their parishes, while a still greater majority admitted to being concerned about the stability of the Catholic Church in general as a result of the scandals. A handful of others expressed the belief that the Church's strength and stability will grow as a result of the allegations. Still others wrote that their parishes were largely untouched by the scandals. In fact, one wrote: "I found the majority of parishioners moved quickly past all this."

4. How concerned are you about the strength and stability of other parishes affected by these allegations of sexual misconduct?

Sixty-nine percent of the responses indicated some concern about other parishes. This was higher than the percentage concerned with their own parishes, leading me to believe that most respondents were not in parishes dealing with allegations against their own priests. This belief is bolstered by the fact that only one respondent acknowledged being placed in his particular parish to fill the void left by a priest removed for alleged sexual misconduct.

More specifically, the majority of respondents (just over 50%) to this question were "somewhat concerned" about *other* parishes rather than the 23% who responded likewise about their own parishes. Only one of the 26 participants answered "not at all concerned" about other parishes (versus eight who answered "not at all concerned" about their own parish).

5. *Have you recently doubted or questioned your choice and commitment to your vocation [priesthood]?*

A resounding 58% of the respondents answered NO, while 23% answered YES. Among those answering YES, there were often personal notations written next to the question. Responses included such things as feeling "extremely overworked," "taxed," "isolated," and "concerned that these scandals will further decrease [new] vocations, making the individual workload of remaining priests hugely difficult." Fifteen percent of the respondents said they simply DON'T KNOW if the scandals have caused them to doubt their chosen vocation.

6. *Have you recently felt more strong and sure about your choice and commitment to your vocation?*

Sixty-nine percent of the respondents answered YES. One priest wrote: "I feel that amidst the crisis, my service has become more rewarding in as much as it helps to work against the scandal." Other responses included:

> "I feel good about doing my best to help this situation."

> "This work gives my vocation new meaning."

and

"It is important to combat that which threatens the Church's mission."

Generally, the reactions to this question demonstrated the belief in a worthy, meaningful and inspirational cause.

Only 8% of the priests questioned responded NO, though many of these respondents included passionate handwritten comments about their emotional turmoil, uncertainty, anger, and bitterness towards the current events (and the effect those events have had on some priests' certainty of vocation choice). One priest wrote: "I need either *more* or *less* — I mean that in coming years, unless something positive happens to relieve the stress I experience each day, I can see myself applying to a monastery to gain some peace (more) or requesting a leave of absence leading to laitization (less)."

Fifteen percent of the respondents answered DON'T KNOW to this question.

7. *In the wake of the recent allegations and subsequent removals of clergy, have you felt less-trusted or treated with more caution or suspicion by your parishioners?*

Over one quarter of the respondents (27%) acknowledged feeling less trusted and/or being treated suspiciously by parishioners. Thirty-nine percent felt otherwise, while 35% said they were unsure.

One priest commented: "I *feel* or *sense* more mistrust but can really not be certain."

Many of the respondents wrote that parishioner reticence is reasonable and should be expected by clergymen.

8. How much of your work do you feel needs to be focused on building trust and alleviating fears with your parishioners?

Only one priest replied that *all* of his work needed to be focused on building trust and alleviating fear in his congregation, while 8% felt that *most* of their work needed to be concentrated here and 8% were unsure of how much focused attention was required.

One comment read: "Most work must be here now lest we lose those who may be 'on the fence'." While another cautioned:

> "Only *some* of the work of the clergy should be placed here as we must not lose focus on what we are here for — to concentrate and deliver God's message."

9. Do you feel there is a clear solution to dealing with this issue of priest sexual misconduct?

The responses to this question were neck-and-neck, with 35% responding YES, 35% NO, and 31% DON'T KNOW. One respondent complained that it was "impossible to answer such a question in one word." Others agreed that it was "hard to decide between yes and no." This belief likely explains the large number of DON'T KNOW responses. In retrospect, I would have phrased this question differently or added a specific response area to accompany this question. My sense is that the responses here were "loaded."

Several priests gave ideas on how they felt these incidents should be handled, including:

> "We need more vigilance and greater concern for responding to possible misdeeds."

> "We need strict enforcement of Church rules disallowing these sorts of activities to take place."

and

> "Swifter removal of alleged perpetrators."

Two respondents emphasized the need for the Church to institute far stricter ordination requirements. One even alleged that "degenerates are deliberately infiltrated into the seminaries and worthy candidates excluded in their place."

10. *Do you feel there is adequate energy and movement toward that direction [dealing with the issue of priest misconduct] by the Catholic Church?*

Fifty-eight percent of the respondents answered YES, with two such respondents expressing the belief that *too much* attention and movement was focused on these events. Twelve percent of the priests surveyed answered NO, and 31% said they were unsure.

OTHER THEMES

Interest in project and appreciation for an avenue to contribute.

Many of the priests participating in the study thanked me for embarking on this exploration and for valuing their stories and insights. One note read: "Your work will be helpful to many who are struggling." Another read: "I think your venture is a good one", and then went on to highlight the questions and areas in the cover letter that he felt had special impact and were important. Another (via telephone) said simply: "Thank you for listening to what I have to say."

Overall, I was surprised to find many of the participants grateful to have been offered a forum to express their opinions and experiences. And they did so with a fervor and honesty that impressed me greatly.

Anger

Another theme that emerged from this study was that of anger and bitterness.

> "I am angry at the anger of the parishioners because I do not deserve this treatment...."

> "[I am] angry about being judged and not being

viewed as an individual."

Several responses indicated anger with how poorly the Church handled the reported sexual abuse claims. One respondent wrote of his anger with Church authorities who felt they could "turn the other way" or "conveniently be blinking" when the alleged incidents were happening. A few priests reported feeling anger and frustration that deviants were not discovered earlier. And one participant expressed skepticism that the Church's gatekeepers would be able to weed out and properly handle individuals "seeking ordination for less than stellar reasons."

The US Conference of Catholic Bishops has also highlighted the poor screening practices of seminaries interviewing candidates for the priesthood and has blamed these practices for contributing to the widespread incidence of abuse. Robert Bennett, the Washington attorney who headed the task force behind a recent study on the sex abuse allegations, agrees that "dioceses simply did not screen candidates for priesthood properly."

But Church officials weren't the only targets of respondents' anger. Several priests wrote or spoke of their anger with Church therapists and lawyers. One insightful respondent wrote:

> Look back in history. Look to when these allegations were first arising. Look to the therapists and lawyers who came forward with victims. They were first to point fingers, but slow to lend support and guidance. For many years, the Church was operating out of their league, out of their expertise. Only in recent years has the Church been advised

properly on these sexual disorders. Only recently
have the Church authorities begun to understand the
repeat rates of pedophiles. Only now do we know
that these individuals cannot be moved to another
parish, they cannot be given a fresh start or another
chance.

Another responded similarly:

Back when these crimes were first being committed
in the churches, who knew what pedophilia was or
how to handle it? The Church's counsel was by
therapists and lawyers, each with their own ideas of
how to deal with these events. Looking back, it was
the lawyers advocating for laying low, moving and
hiding these perpetrators for their own good and
that of the Catholic Church. And the therapists
forgot to tell us about the recidivism rates of
pedophiles. You just can't move these men to new
surroundings to cure what ails them, so to speak.

One respondent said he was angry that the Church trusted
"those outsiders who claimed to know what was best for the
Church." Another said he knew of Church officials pressured by
their legal counsel to "handle these issues within the closed
community of the Church."

The Church's apparent evasiveness when cornered on the
issue also drew ire from some respondents. There was a general
consensus that "straight forwardness" and "honesty" were most
appreciated by parishioners trying to deal with the recent wave of
crises. One priest wrote:

People are set free when they hear the truth, spoken with conviction and love. It resonates within them and they get emotional balance and freedom in their thinking, which has been confused by the crisis.

On a slightly different note, two respondents expressed anger and resentment about what they perceive as a large-scale endeavor to damage their Church and calling:

The clerical sex scandals we see are part of a plan to discredit the Catholic Church.

The priest has been made a symbol not only of impurity but sexual perversity as well.

There was a feel of defensiveness and bitterness to these priests' responses. One priest labeled those who've come out vocally against the Church as "critics of the Church who shout hypocrisy too loudly."

All who responded with angry sentiment agreed that perpetrators of sexual crimes should be held accountable for their actions. And blame was firmly attached to those who violated their vows and abused their position as clergy. In particular, one respondent wrote: "I am shocked and angry at the priests who failed to respect their vow of celibacy and failed to get help when they realized they had a problem." All respondents who wrote or commented on this topic agreed that in *any* case of substantiated sexual misconduct by a priest, that priest should immediately be removed, swiftly dealt with, and not transferred to any other parish or organization.

Sexuality / Should Catholic priests be allowed to marry?

Many clergy focused on this area in their comments, all of whom felt the suggestion that allowing priests to marry would solve the Church's problems is, by itself, entirely too simplistic of a possession.

> Yes, married priests might help a bit, but [more importantly] we need holy and righteous priests [regardless of their marital status]. Protestant ministers and Rabbis have their sexual misconduct problems too.

> The sexual perversity is a commentary on people today. It is a more common occurrence in the general population these days, not simply a symptom stemming from priests' vow of celibacy.

> Marriage is not what these [accused] clergy are wanting or looking for — this is evident in that the sacrament [of marriage] is not granted between men and minor boys.

This last comment may prove particularly insightful, as the just-released in-depth research study by John Jay College of Criminal Justice seems to indicate. It reports that indeed, the vast majority of victims of these alleged incidents were males between the ages of eleven and seventeen. The argument here is that a grown man's sexual interest in young boys is unlikely to be influenced by whether or not he was permitted to marry.

Further, as one priest added:

> We cannot assume that these [accused] priests are in
> fact keeping their vows of celibacy if they are
> clearly breaking other legal and moral rules and
> vows.

This point struck me. Indeed, looking at the simple vow of celibacy as being a major consequence of entering the priesthood is a large assumption on our part. Not only do we not know how the celibate life affects practicing clergy, but we also do not know how many are actually keeping this vow.

In regards to priests and sexuality, I was granted several conversations with participants about this topic. The discussions were fascinating. I have always wondered about the celibate experience of priests, but I've been too frightened to ask. Until, that is, the priests I spoke with for this book were so honest and forthcoming that I felt okay bringing up the topic.

The consensus was that the commitment to a celibate life was certainly one of the more difficult vows to take and keep over the course of one's vocation. However, two priests wrote of providing counsel to countless parish couples over the years where sexual relations had been non-existent for longer than the priests had been celibate. Reasons for the lack of sexual intercourse in these relationships ranged from physical illness and depression to marital unhappiness and discord.

Perhaps most interesting was that the priests I spoke with

described a deep, non-physical intimacy through other occurrences in their careers. One priest spoke of several relationships with non-clergy women (and on occasion, nuns) that were the closest and most intimate he had ever experienced. Yet they remained entirely non-physical in nature. "These were women," he said, "that in another life I would have fallen in love with, married, and had a family with."

A couple of the priests explained a profoundly deep level of intimacy through prayer, either alone or with a woman close to them. A few spoke to the fact that there was a "strong commitment to and respect for a priest's vocation" and that this aided them in not acting on something [sexual activity] that might jeopardize that vocation.

Two priests (identifying themselves as joining the priesthood "later in life") felt that they had simply reached a point in their lives where they could handle celibacy. These respondents were yearning for more deeply satisfying experiences in their lives. True to the psychological developmental stages of middle and later adulthood, older men often contemplate their past choices, their generativity — Have I been a good father? Husband? Have I accomplished my goals? Have I achieved all I wanted from my career? These sorts of questions help them to gauge their importance/self-worth. And during this period of a man's life, sexuality is often not the primary focus.

One priest relayed his view that most priests lack the "marriage temperament." That is to say, that after experiencing the life of a priest, it is difficult (if not impossible) to enjoy the full scope of a layperson's relationship. "Hence, the high failure rate of ex-priests' marriages," he explains. After the end of such relationships, "some will return to the priesthood and some will not, going on to countless other failed relationships and marriages."[1]

A couple of clergy members strongly pressed their opinions that marriage and celibacy are completely unrelated to the sex scandals. In other words, they felt "pedophilia and other unnatural sexual acts were most often perpetrated by those who were sexually active and often in marriages, not celibate and married to God." One response was:

> Some ask, "What came first, the chicken or the egg?" when speaking of whether the criminal came into the Church, or the Church created the criminal — there is no such dilemma. The criminal came into the Church, not the other way around.

Another priest felt "these unfortunate events were just that – terribly unfortunate – but plainly not due to a priest's vow of celibacy."

A few respondents agreed to speak with me about past screening protocol for seminarian students seeking ordination. One priest claims to specifically focus on issues of sexuality in the course of interviews. This focus might include such questions as:

---

[1] Despite this priest's view, it appears that the failure rate of post-priesthood relationships and marriages among priests who have left the ministry closely mirrors the statistics in the general population.

Do you have sexual feelings?

Is masturbation a part of your life?

and

How do you manage feelings of physical attraction
to someone?

Some respondents felt this was vital information to have about
priest candidates, although many admitted that they were not often
so direct in their questioning.

One respondent argues that *whether* a candidate has ever had
sexual relations is far less important than *when* he last had such
relations:

> If a candidate tells me he has had sex with women
> over the years, I am not alarmed, although if the last
> time he enjoyed such sexual activity was yesterday
> afternoon, it is more of an issue in my mind!

Others said they would be far more alarmed by a candidate who
claimed no sexual activity or interest than one who felt attraction
and sexuality but was determined to manage them in order to fulfill
their vocation. One priest relayed this hilarious tale:

> Whenever Saint Francis has sexual feelings, he
> stripped naked, marched himself outside, and threw
> himself into the snow!

Another offered:

> What is worse? A priest who has managed his physical sexuality through occasional masturbation or one who has sought out his sexual perversity on innocent young boys? In my opinion, a fault of masturbation is a human error that is between the priest and God and hurts no one.

One area of responses centered on homosexuality and the priesthood. Several priests spoke of the need to "distinguish between gay priests and pedophile priests." Another described a "don't ask/don't tell attitude" that he felt existed within the Church community. In the end, of the priests that commented on the topic, *all* felt that a gay priest was completely acceptable as long as he maintained his vow of celibacy. One participant, in particular, said:

> I am completely comfortable with the notion of a self-recognized homosexual being ordained, assuming he feels he can be in control of his desires, and also assuming he is not seeking out the priesthood as a forum to find a community of men who are living together and may provide sexual outlets for said priest.

Others agreed that homosexuality, when not being physically acted upon, is not determinative of whether a priest can fulfill his duties. One such response was:

> A priest's mission necessitates a celibate life... Regardless of his sexual orientation, a priest must remain focused on the vows he has taken, including

to not have sexual relations. My fear is that some may enter the priesthood thinking it will act as a shroud for a subculture of homosexual behavior.

Another interesting area of responses fell in the realm of what one priest called the "immature sexuality" of some priesthood candidates. He described these candidates as "appearing to be inhumanly asexual." In other words, there are a number of men seeking ordination who report having no sexual feelings or attractions whatsoever. One might first think these individuals would be perfect candidates for the priesthood. However, the priests with whom I spoke felt that natural sexuality was far more desirable in a candidate than none at all. One priest likened celibacy to a faithful marriage:

> From the beginning, temptation has always existed. In a faithful marital union, the partners must endure these temptations and remain committed and true. Priests must also weather temptation and remain faithful to their vows.

There are a variety of opinions regarding homosexuality, marriage, and celibacy in the priesthood, leaving plenty to debate and hash out. But, in the end, there appears to be a sturdy stance among clergy members that the issue of married priests is not germane to the Church's sexual misconduct problems. As one interviewee wrote:

> Allowing a priest to take a wife will not put an end to the chance of a molester infiltrating the ministry,

as that molester is not looking for a wife or even a sexual act with a woman, but rather a young child.

Isolation

Many responses pointed to feeling abandoned by, and/or isolated from, others as a result of the scandals. Some priests said they felt "distrusted and abandoned by parishioners;" others expressed apprehension about being wrongfully caught in a web of suspicion because of the Church's recently instituted "zero tolerance" policy. One clergyman, in particular, offered: "I find myself isolated from clergy and laity alike."

If priests cannot confide in or talk with others close to them about their concerns, how will they then be empowered to seek out help and guidance when needed? And if there are not healthy channels of communication between priests and the more administrative positions in the Church, how can there be a collaborative effort to avoid more scandals?

A few of the priests I surveyed suggested that some in the congregation seemed to fear them; that there was a "them versus us divide" apparent in certain situations. These respondents felt sad and frustrated that some parishioners seem to view them as "unapproachable," thus further isolating the priest(s) (or at least increasing the priests' sense of isolation).

Some respondents spoke of their anger towards poorly handled situations by other clergy as being a reason for their feelings of isolation. In other words, the discomfort with certain

Church leaders made some priests withdraw from group gatherings with other clergy and Church officials. One participant wrote:

> I refuse to attend vicariate meetings, clergy days of recollection and study, and only attend events that are absolutely mandatory.

Another penned:

> I am in all functionally pertinent ways, alienated from the religious hierarchy.

Yet another wrote:

> I tend to avoid many of the group meetings that I anticipate will leave me in unsettled turmoil.

Ironically, these priests' response to the scandals – i.e., to withdraw from the Church's larger clergy community – only lengthens and deepens their periods of despondency and feelings of isolation.

Undoubtedly, the nature of clergy life is, in itself, somewhat isolated. Priests usually live alone or with another priest. They are often asked to relocate or take over duties in nearby parishes, leaving them unable to lay down roots. I inquired about the constant changing of priests in the parishes — was this shuffling around designed to shield priests suspected of deviant behavior? After all, it's hard to tell from the outside looking in. But most respondents answered NO to this question. One, in particular, wrote:

> The moves are for the good of the priests as well as for the parishioners so that there is no staleness. Priests should not become too connected or at home in any parish, lest they become stagnant and unwilling to go away when their service might be needed elsewhere.

Another offered:

> This flexibility and fluidity of priests makes it easier to fill vacancies and quickly position help wherever it may be needed, especially in this time of priest shortages.

There are certain sects of monks that take an extra vow to their community ("stability to property"), thus enabling them to remain in one place for life. But the respondents resoundingly answered that the majority of priests will – and should – be rotated. This, despite the loneliness that accompanies the constant moves.

Dealing With the Isolation

One priest explained that most clergy are aware of the "occupational hazard of isolation" inherent in their vocation. As with any other job, some parts are less desirable than others. How well each individual priest deals with this isolation varies.

Given the circumstances that appear to isolate priests from many types of relationships, how do practicing priests cope with this isolation? Many respondents reported that their families were very important to them and one of the biggest support systems in their lives. One priest explained:

> I save up for a two-week trip each year to visit my family no matter where I might be at the time. It is very important to me to maintain family relationships. My family treats me like everyone else, which is rarely the case with my parish — it is the one place where my Mother will ask if I'm getting enough to eat and if I've been to the doctor for check-ups!

A couple of priests remarked on how their siblings "shared" their own children with them so that, at times, nieces and nephews seemed like their own children. In fact, due to his high familial involvement, one priest claimed he "never really missed having children [of his own]." Others said their parishes served as excellent "foster families."

In addition to family, a required part of the priesthood is that each priest choose and utilize a spiritual advisor (sometimes known as a "spiritual director" or "confessor"). This person serves as a confidante to the priest. The advisor's identity is kept completely confidential, as is anything that is discussed between the two. *Who* a priest chooses can be quite diverse. One priest I spoke with had chosen a female (non-Catholic) ordained minister. Another respondent told me he used a psychotherapist as his advisor. "Whoever is chosen," one priest told me, the advisor "should be someone the priest feels he can trust and who will help him with struggles." In this regard, these advisors can be very helpful in combating loneliness and isolation.

A few priests spoke or wrote of "mutual support groups" — individuals drawn from various professions (e.g., clergy, lawyers) that meet to help one another with job-related stress. Other types of groups are sometimes created as well, such as meetings of clergy from different faiths that gather to discuss current events and issues within their congregations or communities. One priest consistently schedules these sorts of groups and meetings every other week. One respondent felt so strongly about this endeavor that he cautioned: "those who do not seek out such group support are heading for a crash landing."

Others have found company in the homes of parishioners where they are sometimes invited for dinner or other functions.

Although these are some ways that priests find companionship, one of the most important relationships they will likely have is with the other priest(s) in their parish. "A strong relationship is almost inevitable when priests must share living space, eat together, and work together," one priest wrote. However, if the priests find themselves to be incompatible or to otherwise have a strained relationship, it can be a source of great distress.

One participant in this study recounted the story of two priests who had a "terrible, argumentative relationship." The two repeatedly attempted to "make it work," but failed miserably. They finally went to their superiors, who tried to help the pair mediate their differences. "In the end," though, "the attempts were futile and one of the priests was relieved to be placed in another state."

A few respondents spoke of the relationship between parish priests as being similar to a marriage. One said: "Priests must navigate the personalities, habits, and quirks of one another and wrestle with them just as any other couple would have to do." The majority of priests seem to lean heavily on one another and therefore, a good, compatible, and respectful relationship is vital.

Another interesting theme that arose from the participants' responses dealt with the priests' relationships with the laity. One priest felt "warmly welcomed and comfortable" with his parishioners, and had "wonderful relationships and friendships" with them. A handful of others expressed feeling accepted by and comfortable with members of their parish, but found it more difficult to have serious relationships with them. One priest stated:

> A priest is kidding himself if he thinks he can have a "normal" relationship with the laity. There is a stigma that remains of what a priest is supposed to be. Certain ideals and expectations still exist. What would the parishioners think if Father John Doe decided to have fun gambling at the casino one night? Ooh, Ooh, Father laughed at a dirty joke… Only those in the priesthood can truly understand the experience.

Another agreed that "regular relationships are hard to come by when you are a priest." One priest said:

> There are always things you can never do in front of

others [laity]. A priest has to have a guard up. He has to be careful what he says and does or it might be seen as scandalous.

One priest likened a priest's relationship with the laity to being a celebrity:

> They're watching everything you do, putting you on an idealistic pedestal. The constant judgment and scrutiny takes a toll on you.

Coping with the Priest Shortage

There was definitely a thread of concern woven into priests' responses about this subject. Some of the respondents expressed feeling overwhelmed by the additional workload placed on them due to a general priest shortage. Many are concerned that this trend will get worse. One priest spoke of the recent closing of churches:

> I am greatly concerned by these closings. Are these parishes closing due to a shortage of priests? Or… because of the legal ramifications of the sexual abuse cases? We have not been told and are therefore concerned about the unknown — just how much is the shortage affecting the churches? And where will all those parishioners go to worship?

One of the greatest concerns about the shortage of new priests is its potential to further isolate current priests. One respondent described seeing "more and more parishes with only one priest" —

leaving the entire workload to one priest living alone amongst parishioners. Priests living alone can be a problem in itself, according to many of the respondents — one of whom explained that some religious orders (e.g., The Franciscans) openly oppose their priests living alone and are strong activists for the socialization of priests.

Feeling isolated and alone can lead to outlet behaviors like alcohol and drug abuse — an all-too-common reality of priesthood life. In fact, one priest went so far as to say:

> I believe the prevalence of alcoholism in the priesthood is far greater than the incidence of sexual abuse in the Church.

Several others spoke of priests being temporarily removed from their parishes for alcohol and/or drug treatment. As was the case with a priest "who showed up completely drunk and slurring to do a baptism", some priests are sent for treatment. Others self-refer themselves to treatment. Still others, however, consider alcohol use necessary to bear the depths of their depression.

Some of the respondents believe the shortage of priests is an inevitability of modern life. So much so that they say it shouldn't be an issue of discussion. Consider this response from one priest:

> The priesthood is not such a revered and enticing career choice anymore — it is merely a sign of the times. The Church is simply dealing with the limited number of priests by doling out many duties to laypeople in order to get the work done. It will continue in this manner as long as there are fewer

new priests and a growing population of Catholics.

Others agreed that deacons, parish secretaries, catechists, and Eucharistic lay ministers are now commonly doing tasks that priests used to do. One priest freely offered that his parish secretaries "handle and control just about everything." Volunteers are often solicited in the Church under a recently instituted policy of "declericalization."[*] Most respondents felt that heavy layperson involvement in the Church was appropriate and necessary. One priest offered this caution, however:

> Take note that not all of the perpetrators of sexual abuse in the Catholic Church were ordained priests. A small number of the abusers were deacons, seminarians, and various other non-ordained persons. The current trend of layperson involvement in the Church can be both a Godsend and a potential liability. We must proceed with caution.

Forgiveness

One especially fitting theme in this study was the notion of forgiveness. One clergy member emphasized that, "Forgiveness is at the heart of our Christian way of life." Another agreed: "We must not lose sight of forgiveness." "We must be careful not to

---

[*] AUTHOR NOTE: My own parish is now requiring each registered family to volunteer for at least one Church activity — an extensive list that ranges from simple tasks like baking for retreats or being a "prayer friend" to more time consuming choices like office/computer work or singing in the Church choir.

become righteous and judge others," warned still another.

One response pointed to the image of the "pearly gates of Heaven":

> All shall be judged at the doorway to paradise. At the pearly gates of Heaven, each man shall meet his maker. Then, and only then, shall he be allowed or disallowed an eternity with the Lord. Each man alone with his actions on the Lord's doorstep. Up until that very moment, forgiveness may be granted.

Another priest felt that:

> The beauty of our faith and our God's commandments are at the center here... We humble humans should not cast the first stone at another. Rather that we humans allow the almighty to pass Judgment.

Many of the participants in this study referred to a similar vein of thought — their advice to people wanting to find closure and healing is to forgive. One priest, in particular, wrote:

> One of His 12 apostles denied him and yet another betrayed him. Still, the Lord found forgiveness in his heart.

A struggle to strength

> I feel it is a sign of God's love whenever the Church is called to greater holiness and authenticity. I think this belief and sentiment should be remembered by

the many who struggle with the state of things, and hopefully this will be helpful in healing them.
– A Respondent Priest

One priest wrote:

Many of these [sexual misconduct] cases occurred at a time in the life of the Church and our society when there was much theological/moral confusion. We are reaping the bitter fruits of that era.

But many respondents feel the recent Church crises and struggles have created a greater strength and cohesion among Church members. As one priest put it:

The positive side of all this however, is that I am a wiser person who has been strengthened by those who love and support me."

Another offered:

The great growth of faith of the people through all of this has not only been impressive but also inspiring.

Still others wrote:

Many parishioners have admitted that they have had to reevaluate their faith and as a result are now stronger Catholics.

The Lord is 'cleaning house'. He is hearing the prayers of many who have been longing for a purified clergy and Church.

and

Although this may be a painful time, it is also a hopeful time of restoration and reformation.

The human element

The influence of human weakness on the priesthood littered the sundry responses. One clergyman, in particular, offered a wealth of information on the topic. I have inset his three central points here:

> 1. Part of each of us is "animal." Those who choose the priesthood are often choosing a road in religion to stay on track and to keep these animal instincts in check.

> 2. We are each walking in the muck of our humanity, trying to raise ourselves up above it. [The choice of vocation] is one way to do this.

> 3. We [the clergy] are a human institution grappling with our divine mandate every moment of every day. Sometimes we succeed, and sometimes we do not.

The respondents encourage believers to "stay focused on Jesus Christ as the center of our Church (rather than on the clergy)," and to "be a strong and faithful witness to Jesus Christ and His gospel."

Others expressed a need to help "people to direct their faith to God and not to priests", and to assist "those with a weak faith who have put all their hope in priests and the institutional Church."

One respondent advised:

> Many would be encouraged by meeting the priests, deacons, and lay leaders whose faith is firm in Christ and his sacraments.

While recognizing the fallibility of mankind and every institution depending upon it (including the Church), many of the priests expressed a hope that we will "focus on the vast majority of good and faithful shepherds of the Lord."

The media

There is no doubt that the media has taken an extreme interest in covering and sensationalizing the crisis. The majority of comments offered in this area agreed that the media was a "dual-edged sword." On one side, the coverage has sliced through the secrecy and brought forth the hidden scandals, allowing the problem to be acknowledged, addressed, and dealt with. It has also reinforced in the minds of the many victims that what happened to them was wrong, and has made them more comfortable seeking out support and assistance.

Generally, the respondents concur: "the press and media in general have been helpful in uncovering the problem" and in "disallowing the shrouding of these problems." One priest wrote: "I am grateful, as we all should be, that the media brought these issues to the forefront. They did the right thing."

However, there is another side to the media's probing and reporting. "The press has often hyped the problem and caused some to lose balance and perspective," writes one respondent. Another priest agreed, adding: "Sometimes the focus is entirely too much on the deviance and not enough on the vast majority of sincerity and goodness." Others echoed this concern. For example, one priest wrote:

> The media always goes to one, the abuser, and two, to those who covered up the alleged events. What about all the rest of us who are not committing such horrific things? For each isolated allegation, there are hundreds others who are good and trustworthy. And no one wants to speak with us.

One clergyman wrote of his disgust "[when a certain talk show host] did a show on children who had been abused by priests on Holy Thursday." He expressed his irritation with the "lack of sensitivity and respect" shown by airing the show on a Catholic holy day.

Will it happen again?

Many of the participants in this study felt that sexual misdeeds like these will not happen again. Most wrote that too much focus and scrutiny has been placed on priests to let any future abuses "slip by undetected." Others agreed that "if anything, even innocent priests are being looked at with doubt, watched closely, and scrutinized."

The Church has hired an outside firm to screen every practicing priest and anyone attempting to volunteer or work within the Church establishment. This includes (as one respondent put it) "the volunteer in the soup kitchen and the Bingo caller." Describing this evaluation, one priest wrote:

> The screenings are the most in-depth and thorough ones that exist today. This is to make sure that the atrocities that have occurred cannot happen again. In fact, other institutions should follow the lead and implement such checks with their employees. Abuse occurs in schools and other places as well....

Another clergyman said:

> This intricate system of checks and balances will uncover anyone who does not belong in the role they are seeking. Those with sordid and sullied histories and those with potential malintent will be immediately removed. Even the medical and educational communities have not yet implemented such a thorough measure.

Still another added:

> I believe the Church is, and has always been, one of the safest places for children. These unfortunate events will not be tolerated again. It says something

that the Bishops themselves are the ones requesting these intense studies and background checks.

In complement to these third-party investigations, the review of men studying to become priests has been beefed up significantly. Looking for signs of "sexual abnormality" is now encouraged, as is a rigorous exploration of sexual thoughts and practices, including explicit questions about sexual feelings, physical attraction, and masturbation.

The other priests' responses notwithstanding, there were two respondents who ardently disagreed with the position that sexual abuse by priests would never happen again. These two were skeptical of any screening methods that would definitively point to pedophilia or other sexual aberrance. One argued:

> How does one successfully screen for sexual deviance? People can lie, omit, or be selective with what they say. If we had a 100% effective way to find sexual deviants, we wouldn't have any of them in the Church.

Another priest restated and expanded this position, writing:

> Just recently, a young girl was snatched in broad daylight from a crowded area, sexually abused, and killed. Although people were aware of the current dangers, this terrible thing happened anyway. No one could prevent it. No one stopped it. It happened. And it will happen again. It could happen again in the Church as well.

FOLLOW-UP INTERVIEWS

After completing my research and summarizing the findings, I attempted to contact a dozen priests from my original list. My intent was to share the results of this study and get some feedback.

Again, I chose names randomly from my original list. So I didn't know if the priests I called were ones who had participated in this endeavor, or if they were part of the 59% that did not. I was able to reach eleven of the selected priests. Nine of them agreed to speak with me. The other two declined.

Several of the follow-up phone interviews lasted more than half an hour. Others were slightly shorter due to the priest's already-scheduled appointments and obligations.

While apparently as surprised as I at the high response rate from queried priests, the consensus among these nine priests was that, despite fear of reprisal from Church hire-ups for speaking out, clergymen are "generally quite hungry for the opportunity to speak and be listened to." Additionally, one priest felt that "due to past experiences with the media, many of the clergy may feel distrusting and wary of outsiders [asking questions]." Another interviewee shared that many of his colleagues "felt enough was written and said about the scandals" and that they "knew enough about it to move past it" (and were now "tired of talking about it all)." Another commented that "it is an internal issue now" and it "need not be explored further by media and laity."

Overall, the priests I spoke with agreed with the study's findings. They were not surprised by the diversity in responses, nor were they shocked by some of the more candid comments.

HOW DO WE PROTECT OUR CHILDREN?

At least 3% to 7% of all boys are abused sexually by the time they reach eighteen. Scores more girls face a similar crisis. The problems are not confined within Church walls. They extend to every corner of the morally dilapidated society we've created for ourselves. And with this reality in mind, we must be more vigilant with regard to our children than our parents were with us.

Here are some suggestions on keeping your child safe:

Keep the lines of communication open with your children.

Do not be afraid to talk with your kids about current events, including disturbing happenings like child abductions and sexual abuse within the Church. It is crucial that they are aware, at least peripherally, of the dangers that might otherwise be hidden to them. There are age-specific guidelines that should be followed, of course. But more importantly, parents should take into account a child's maturity and development when deciding which discussion topics and details are appropriate.

Don't be afraid to ask questions. And check up on your kids. They may feign frustration, and claim that you're "spying" on them, but don't let this dissuade you. They are your kids, and they're in your charge. They will ultimately recognize the monitoring as an act of love and not a needless intrusion into their private space and time.

Perhaps most importantly, be an active listener when your kids make time to talk with you. It is the best way to gain their trust and encourage future dialogues.

Keep the lines of communication open with other adults.

Keep connected with the other adults your children deal with frequently. Be involved at school, church, and in your children's other activities. Get to know the individuals who teach and work with your kids. And seek out the experiences of other parents who have dealt with these individuals. You can never have too much knowledge when it comes to protecting your children.

Trust your gut.

Feelings and intuitions can be very important. Educate your children on dealing with situations and circumstances that make them uncomfortable. Over 21% of the priests who were accused of sexually abusing children were identified as "having boundary issues" by the Church's governing bodies (as reported by John Jay College of Criminal Justice, 2004). If you sense that a priest, or any other adult in your child's life is doing or saying something that crosses a boundary or infringes on your comfort zone or that of your children, consider addressing it directly with that person.

And take note of any strange behaviors you see in priests or other adults in your child's life. Anxiety, personality disorders, depression, and alcohol/drug abuse are often found to coexist with sexual misconduct. Unusual behaviors and such things as slurred speech, alcohol frequently on the breath, flat affect, or inappropriate or excessive touching or attention to a child should be reported at once.

Don't assume it won't happen in your community.

One of the biggest mistakes parents make is to let their guard down by thinking that these sorts of crimes wouldn't or couldn't happen in their community. No community is immune. Take the popular, but inaccurate belief, that molesters tend to prey on attention-deprived children from single-parent households. The reality is that almost 80% of reported clergy abuse victims lived with both parents. The most important fact to take from this book and its underlying survey: every child is at risk and every parent must be on-guard.

Monitor your children and look for sudden behavioral changes.

This is an excellent rule of thumb for all parents. Sexual abuse can scar children for life, both physically and emotionally. A childhood history of abuse can cause countless problems later in life, including substance abuse, post-traumatic stress disorder (PTSD), issues in relationships and with self-confidence, sexual problems and fears, low self esteem, and a higher risk of molesting children themselves. *Any* sudden change in your child should be noted and explored.

Here are some things to look out for:

☐ Nightmares or sudden changes in sleep patterns
☐ Bedwetting
☐ Excessive masturbation or sexual play
☐ Asking unusual questions about sex
☐ Excessive interest in sexual content
☐ Gagging
☐ Physical trauma to the anal or genital area
☐ Painful urination or bowel movements
☐ Self mutilation (e.g., cutting, pinching)
☐ Purposeful risk-taking (e.g., running in front of a moving car)
☐ Loss of appetite
☐ Withdrawing from family or friends
☐ Regressive behaviors (e.g., sleeping with a teddy bear, sucking thumb)
☐ Proclamations of self-disgust, self-hatred
☐ Increase in fears, especially of the dark and of particular places
☐ Unusual aggression or specific aggressive behaviors towards family, friends, pets, or even dolls and toys

If you have any concerns about sudden or unusual changes in your child, talk to him or her about it and ask a professional to help you further discern whether you should be abnormally concerned. Also, be sure to let your children know that they can talk to you about anything. They need to feel comfortable talking with you about things they find upsetting; they need to know that you will listen to them calmly and non-judgmentally.

MY EXPERIENCE AND JOURNEY
AS PSYCHOTHERAPIST, AUTHOR AND CATHOLIC

I think it is safe to say that most of us paint Catholic priests with one, broad brush — as though they share the same upbringing, experiences and worldview. The diverse results of this survey loudly pronounce the absurdity of this singular assessment. Catholic priests are like any and every large body of individuals directed toward a unitary goal — simultaneously similar and remarkably different, all at once.

I walk away from this study with the belief that our Catholic clergy needs and deserves more and better support, attention, and understanding from the Church and its laity. The isolation and lack of support and understanding these men feel is, I believe, entirely undeserved and shameful. The vast majority of our priests are dedicated servants of God trying to fulfill an extremely difficult and all-encompassing job description. I respect – and am inspired by – their dedication and devotion. I believe this survey provided the respondent priests with a well-needed and well-received outlet to discuss their experiences, fears and frustrations. This expression needs to continue in one form or another.

I urge everyone who is struggling with these Church crises to discuss your feelings with the priests themselves. It does no good to harbor your frustrations and doubts inside.

In closing, I offer the guidance of our dear Mother Theresa:

> You see in the final analysis, it is between you and God; it was never between you and them anyway.

Suzanne Rosewell is the youngest female partner in the history of her prestigious Wall Street law firm. She's a strong, driven woman with the will to succeed. Then she meets Elias Garner, an enigmatic black Jazz musician who carries an ancient golden trumpet and represents the even more furtive "Chairman" (whom we learn heads the most powerful corporation on earth).

Elias explains that God has always placed among us thirty-six righteous people — each of whom "knows the divine will" and all of which must be accounted for if humanity is to redeem itself. Five are missing from the Chairman's list and Suzanne is asked to set aside her career to search for them. If she fails, it appears that the world cannot exist beyond the sunrise.

Beautifully and thoughtfully phrased throughout, A LITTLE LOWER THAN THE ANGELS is a rare and unique work of great literary and spiritual power.

— **Bookpage**

...available everywhere books are sold...